Favorites for Two

Arrangements by Pete Deneff

Disney characters and artwork © Disney
Disney/Pixar elements © Disney/Pixar

*Based on the "Winnie the Pooh" works, by A.A. Milne and E.H. Shepard

ISBN 978-1-70515-359-8

Visit Hal Leonard Online at
www.halleonard.com

Contact Us:
Hal Leonard
7777 West Bluemound Road
Milwaukee, WI 53213
Email: info@halleonard.com

In Europe contact:
Hal Leonard Europe Limited
42 Wigmore Street
Marylebone, London, W1U 2RN
Email: info@halleonardeurope.com

In Australia contact:
Hal Leonard Australia Pty. Ltd.
4 Lentara Court
Cheltenham, Victoria, 3192 Australia
Email: info@halleonard.com.au

THE BALLAD OF THE LONESOME COWBOY

from TOY STORY 4

TROMBONES

Music and Lyrics by
RANDY NEWMAN

BE OUR GUEST

from BEAUTY AND THE BEAST

TROMBONES

Music by ALAN MENKEN
Lyrics by HOWARD ASHMAN

Moderately, in 2

BELLE
from BEAUTY AND THE BEAST

TROMBONES

Music by ALAN MENKEN
Lyrics by HOWARD ASHMAN

Spiritedly

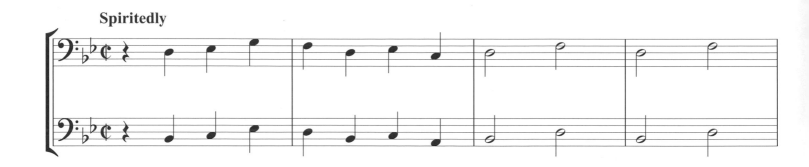

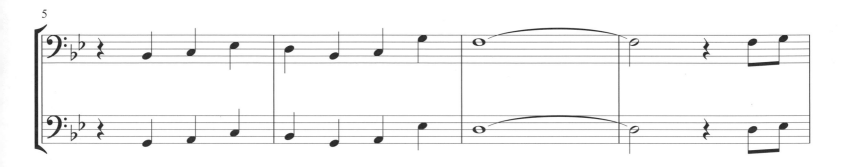

CRUELLA DE VIL
from 101 DALMATIONS

TROMBONES

Words and Music by
MEL LEVEN

A DREAM IS A WISH YOUR HEART MAKES

from CINDERELLA

TROMBONES

Music by MACK DAVID
and AL HOFFMAN
Lyrics by JERRY LIVINGSTON

Moderately

FOR THE FIRST TIME IN FOREVER

from FROZEN

TROMBONES

Music and Lyrics by KRISTEN ANDERSON-LOPEZ
and ROBERT LOPEZ

HOW DOES A MOMENT LAST FOREVER
from BEAUTY AND THE BEAST

TROMBONES

Music by ALAN MENKEN
Lyrics by TIM RICE

IN SUMMER
from FROZEN

TROMBONES

Music and Lyrics by KRISTEN ANDERSON-LOPEZ
and ROBERT LOPEZ

INTO THE UNKNOWN
from FROZEN 2

TROMBONES

Music and Lyrics by KRISTEN ANDERSON-LOPEZ
and ROBERT LOPEZ

JUST AROUND THE RIVERBEND
from POCAHONTAS

TROMBONES

Music by ALAN MENKEN
Lyrics by STEPHEN SCHWARTZ

With motion

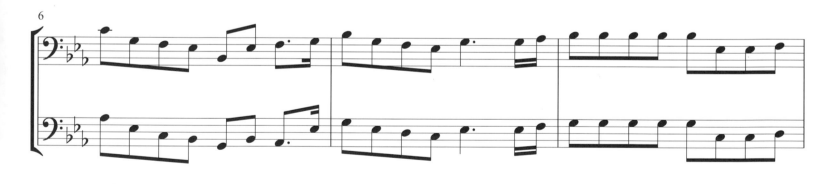

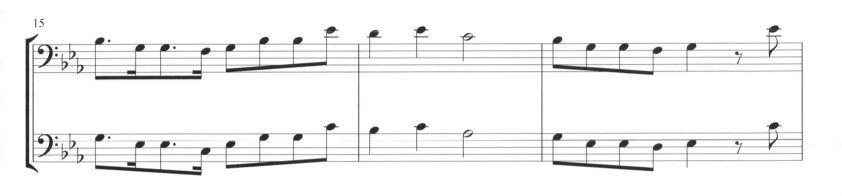

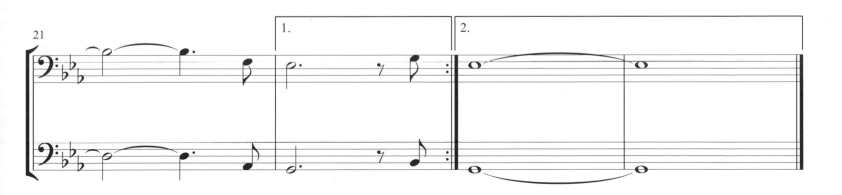

LAVA
from LAVA

TROMBONES

Music and Lyrics by
JAMES FORD MURPHY

Easy half-time feel

LEAD THE WAY

from RAYA AND THE LAST DRAGON

TROMBONES

Music and Lyrics by
JHENÉ AIKO

NEVER TOO LATE
from THE LION KING 2019

Music by ELTON JOHN
Lyrics by TIM RICE

TROMBONES

THE PLACE WHERE LOST THINGS GO

from MARY POPPINS RETURNS

TROMBONES

Music by MARC SHAIMAN
Lyrics by SCOTT WITTMAN
and MARC SHAIMAN

Gently, not slow

REFLECTION
from MULAN

TROMBONES

Music by MATTHEW WILDER
Lyrics by DAVID ZIPPEL

REMEMBER ME
(Ernesto de la Cruz)
from COCO

TROMBONES

Music and Lyrics by KRISTEN ANDERSON-LOPEZ
and ROBERT LOPEZ

Moderately fast

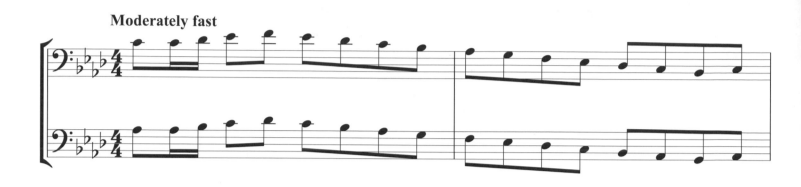

SPEECHLESS
from ALADDIN

TROMBONES

Music by ALAN MENKEN
Lyrics by BENJ PASEK
and JUSTIN PAUL

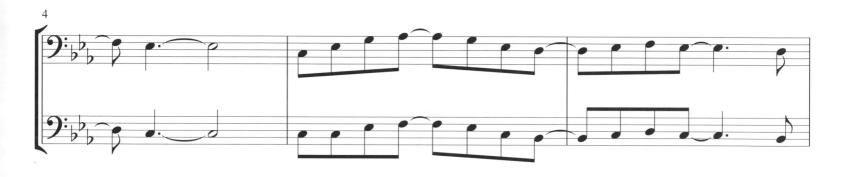

THAT'S HOW YOU KNOW
from ENCHANTED

TROMBONES

Music by ALAN MENKEN
Lyrics by STEPHEN SCHWARTZ

TOUCH THE SKY
from BRAVE

TROMBONES

Music by ALEXANDER L. MANDEL
Lyrics by ALEXANDER L. MANDEL
and MARK ANDREWS

Quickly

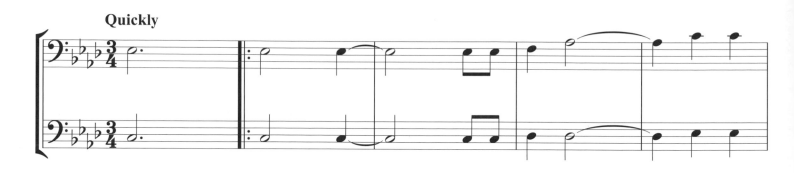

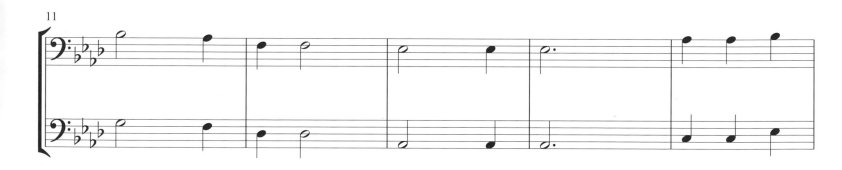

TRY EVERYTHING
from ZOOTOPIA

TROMBONES

Words and Music by SIA FURLER,
TOR ERIK HERMANSEN and MIKKEL ERIKSEN

Moderate Dance beat

UNDER THE SEA
from THE LITTLE MERMAID

TROMBONES

Music by ALAN MENKEN
Lyrics by HOWARD ASHMAN

WINNIE THE POOH
from THE MANY ADVENTURES OF WINNIE THE POOH

TROMBONES

Words and Music by RICHARD M. SHERMAN
and ROBERT B. SHERMAN

YOU'VE GOT A FRIEND IN ME

from TOY STORY

TROMBONES

Music and Lyrics by
RANDY NEWMAN